ALEKSANDR ORLOV

PRESENTS

Bogdan
& THE BIG RACE

MEERKAT CLASSICS

RUSSIA 2012

Bogdan & the Big Race
ALEKSANDR ORLOV

1 3 5 7 9 10 8 6 4 2

First published in 2012 by Ebury Press, an imprint of Ebury Publishing

A Random House Group company

The Random House Group Limited Reg. No. 954009

Addresses for companies within the Random House Group can be found at www.randomhouse.co.uk

A CIP catalogue record for this book is available from the British Library

The Random House Group Limited supports The Forest Stewardship Council (FSC®), the leading international forest certification organisation. Our books carrying the FSC label are printed on FSC® certified paper. FSC is the only forest certification scheme endorsed by the leading environmental organisations, including Greenpeace. Our paper procurement policy can be found at www.randomhouse.co.uk/environment

Printed and bound in Italy by Graphicom SRL

ISBN 9780091950033

To buy books by your favourite authors and register for offers visit www.randomhouse.co.uk

A MESSAGE FROM THE AUTHOR

Hello peoples of UK!

Welcome to another storytelling from Meerkovo. This time we are teaching you how do to arithmetics. Only jokings! Actually we are telling you a tale of great derring-do.

When you read this story of furry-braveness, we hope that you feel a throb of excitement. Because if you are young and small, like hero of this book, you don't always know that you are being taken serious. (Especially if like little Bogdan you are famous for your practical jokings). But if you try very, very hard you will be taken serious and then you can winnings.

My Great Granddaddy Vitaly was always tell me that winnings isn't as important as the playings. Personally I think it is good to both.

Please enjoyment.

Yours,

ALEKSANDR ORLOV

It was **beautiful** sunny day.

All the meerkats of Meerkovo have their sun creams on.
Some of them are wearing sunglasses on their noses.
(If you have not seen meerkats with sunglasses on,
then you are not lookings hard enough).

It was the kind of day when a meerpup who has day
off school feels happy to be alive.

For this is very specials day. It is the final of the

Meerkovian Grand Prix

– the biggest race in all the Russia.
Every famous driver and all the
fastest cars are gathering
together to find out who
is Champion of
Champions.

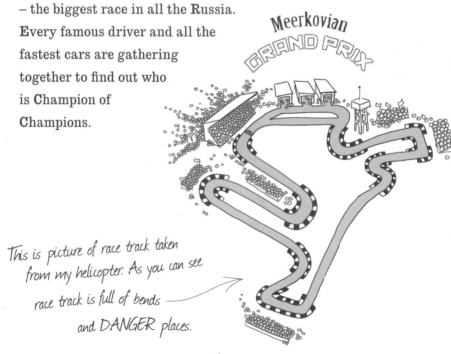

This is picture of race track taken
from my helicopter. As you can see
race track is full of bends
and DANGER places.

The crowd is full of cheering meerpups and their mothers and fathers. Everyone has their packed weevil and termite lunch.* There is excitements everywhere.

On one side of track is villagers of Meerkovo. They are waving special flags that have been claw-stitched by Sergei. (He stayed up all night to make. Which made him very tired and moulty).

On other side of track are the **stinky mongooses.** All the meerkats keep well away from them. As any meerpup will tell you, mongooses are scratchy and full of meanness, and they are the enemy.

*This is very popular Meerkovo snack. It is full of nourishings and is good for thick fur and happy disposition.

Neeeeeeeeeeeaow!*

One by one the cars get behind starting line. Big roar go up.

They are off! **"They're off!"** shout the crowd.

All the cars are painted brightly and look sparkle in the sunshine.

Neeeeeeeeeeeaow! * They go.

Everyone cheered. "Hurrah," they shout. And, just to make sure, "Hurray".

Round corner comes blue car. Then green one, and then yellow one. "All the colours of the rainbow," says wise old meerkat in commentary box. (He is very old and has done many commenting. He always say this about the rainbows).

*You must read this very noisily.
Racing cars are always noise.

Then come mysterious red car.

It is sleek and very fast. It makes roar so mighty the crowd cannot hear itself think. It edge past green car. Then the yellow one. Then it was just behind the blue car.

The crowd gasp and grip the edge of its seat. Who is this mystery driver who is so skill and brave? Nobody know. It is all very puzzlement.

Mystery red car has extra big pipes and number one on it. But otherwise it is typical ultra-modern racing car.

Just then it overtake blue car and is in the lead.

"He is making all the other drivers eat his dust," says wise old meerkat in commentary box.

He is always talking about the dust as well. (Perhaps this is because he is a very dusty wise old meerkat).

Then up goes a shout. **"It's Bogdan!"** It is!

Meerkovo's favourite meerpup. (Despite his prankings, peoples still find him adorables). Everyone jumps up and down in excitements.

Even old Grigor is bouncing up and down in his wheelchair. (Or perhaps he is just forgetting to take his medications).

Then right behind Bogdan's car comes car with big black smoke.

It has evil written all over it.*

*This is a figure of speeches. It does not mean 'evil' was actually written on the car. It mean the car was all nastiness and horridness.

It has push its nose past the yellow and the green
and the blue car until it is just behind the red car.

It is driven by big hairy mongoose who look wicked and
rotten and full of nastiness. He tries to pass Bogdan's
red car but Bogdan too fast.

He try again and even clip wing of
Bogdan's car. Still Bogdan stay ahead.
Then evil mongoose start to play dirty.
He flick a switch and suddenly

spikes come out of his wheels!

The crowd gasp. This is all
very frightenings.

The mongoose come up behind Bogdan
and make his spikes cut into his car.

The crowd now shout and scream in great alarmings.

But somehow Bogdan manage to keep on track.

Then the dirty mongoose make another attack.

This time Bogdan sees it coming and he swerve out of way at last minute. The mongoose car goes flying past and goes straight into barriers.

Big swirly smoke billows out of his car.

The crowd could see the mongoose hopping up and down in a rage and a furiousness.

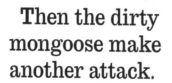

CRASH!

Meanwhile, the red car zoom on to the finishing line. It is way ahead of all other cars.

The chequeredy flag come down with big flourish.

Bogdan is first!

He is winning by 5.5 seconds!

The crowd is beside itself with delightedness.

This diagram reveals secret behind success chequeredy flag-waving. It may look simples, but actually require great skill.

Bogdan is hero!

He climb out of cockpit and is immediately surround by cheering fans.

The race director takes him by the paw and guides him to podium.

There the President of all the Russias congratulate him and hang big medal round his neck. The brass band play Meerkovo Anthem – which is very rousing, and makes the crowd very rouse.

It was wonderful. Bogdan had never feel so proud. (He is sometimes naughty pup, and is no stranger to the dunce's cap, so it is very good for him to be achieving). He could see his mother and father and all his brothers and sisters jumping up and down in the crowd.

Presidents is hold medal ready for presentation. ——→
It is built to giant scale and so heavy
I think he is worry he drop it!

There was **Miss Maiya** his teacher. There was **Vassily**

Miss Maiya

Vassily

and **Great Uncle Grigor.** There was **Sergei** in the pits.

And there was...

Great Uncle Grigor

Sergei

"Bogdan!"

It was the voice of Miss Maiya.

"Bogdan. What have I just been telling you about decimal points? What does 5.5 mean?"

She was standing by blackboard with her special very cross expression.

Bogdan gulped.

He clutched his gleaming red toy car (it was Yakov's finest, and was present from his **Great Uncle Grigor**) and gaze at Miss Maiya. He knows he ought to know about decimal points, somehow he knows it will be important to know one day.

I'm afraid this is not the exercise book of a hard-working pup. He should be writing equations and not illustrating himself.

But just at that moment it isn't mattering.
It may have been a dream, and he may be going straight to
the detention, but Bogdan now know what he is going to be
when he grew up: the fastest racing driver in the whole universe.

Aleksandr's Life Lesson

You must climb every rainbow to make your dreams come true.

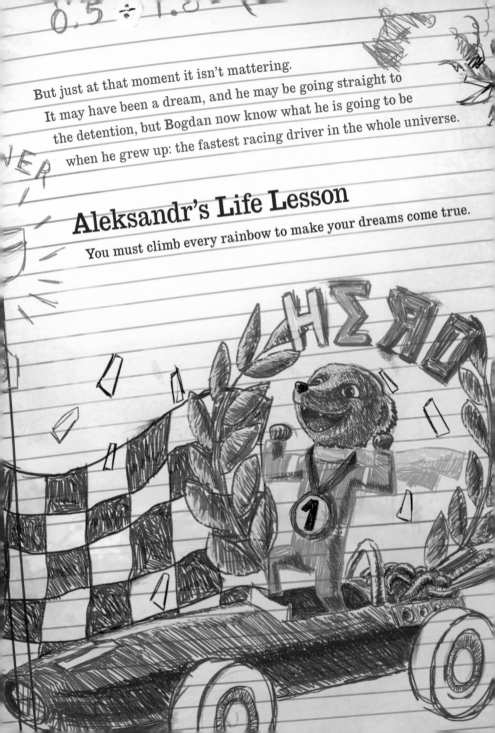

Now read my other greatest tales

Available from all good bookshops

Also available to download as an ebookamabob
or audiomajig as read by the author – me!

For more information visit www.comparethemeerkat.com

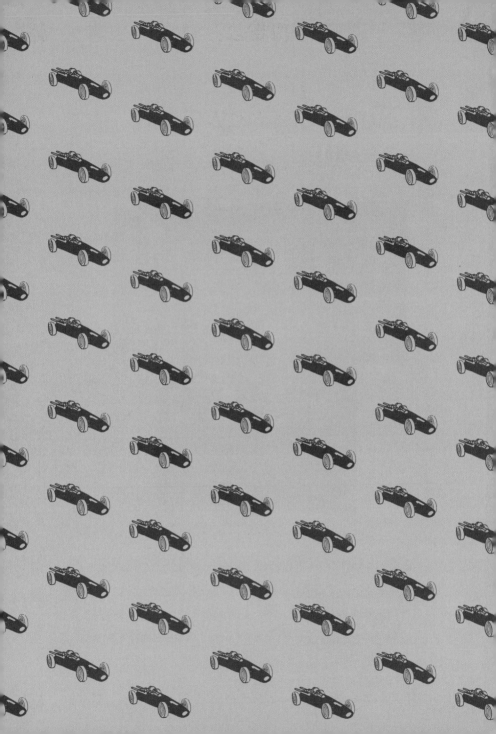

ALEKSANDR ORLOV

PRESENTS

ALEKSANDR

& THE MYSTERIOUS

KNIGHTKAT

MEERKAT
CLASSICS
RUSSIA 2012

Aleksandr & the Mysterious Knightkat
ALEKSANDR ORLOV

1 3 5 7 9 10 8 6 4 2

First published in 2012 by Ebury Press, an imprint of Ebury Publishing

A Random House Group company

This is an advertisement feature on behalf of **comparethemarket**.com

comparethemeerkat.com and **comparethemarket**.com
are trading names of BISL Limited

The Random House Group Limited Reg. No. 954009

Addresses for companies within the Random House Group can be found at www.randomhouse.co.uk

A CIP catalogue record for this book is available from the British Library

The Random House Group Limited supports The Forest Stewardship Council (FSC®), the leading international forest certification organisation. Our books carrying the FSC label are printed on FSC® certified paper. FSC is the only forest certification scheme endorsed by the leading environmental organisations, including Greenpeace. Our paper procurement policy can be found at www.randomhouse.co.uk/environment

Printed and bound in Italy by Graphicom SRL

ISBN 9780091950026

To buy books by your favourite authors and register for offers visit
www.randomhouse.co.uk

This is a work of fiction. Names and characters are the product of the author's imagination and any resemblance to actual persons, living or dead, is entirely coincindental

A MESSAGE FROM THE AUTHOR

Welcome to my bookamabob!

I think you are opening this very special volume with feeling of great excitement. It is the true story of a superhero told by me, Aleksandr.

You already know me as star of stage and screen and semi-successful theatre directings. Now you are see me as writer of literary storytellings!

It has everything you could want in a storytelling: Suspense! Actions! Huge bravenesses! And very importantly a hero of great handsomeness.

Now. Please turn over page and begin...

Yours,

Aleksandr

ALEKSANDR ORLOV

PS: There is hiding in text arithmetic puzzle!
It is on page 20. Answer is at back of book.

It was dark and stormy night.

In mountain village of Meerkovo everywhere was full of raining, and the wind made rattle against the window panes. The sign of the Queasy Mongoose tavern creak and squeak in the howling gale. Everyone was glad to be tucked up in bed.

They didn't know that not far away, in **Orlov** family mansion, there was one who never sleep.

Deep in the heart of the house, behind library and underneath ballroom, was secret dungeon of great enormousness. It was full of flashing computermabobs... and rockets... and super-charged sports cars...

This is south side of Orlov family mansion.
The three giant trees were grown from seed by my Great Granddaddy Vitaly and completely block out light in library!

In the middle of it all were two figures. One was handsome and furry and wearing a red gown. The other was small and grey and scratching himself.

The handsome one was sip his ladybird tea and **thinking great thoughts.*** The grey one was trying to mend his Walkman, in between picking out the fleas from behind his ears.

*We do not know exactly what these thoughts were but we can be sure they were great.

This was secret lair of **Knightkat**, superhero of all Russia, and deadly enemy of evil **Doctor Robogoose,**

the cruellest mongoose villain in the world. (He get his name because he half

robot, half mongoose, which make him stinky metal scoundrel).

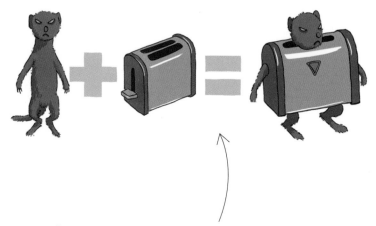

Illustration of science principle: fur+metal=villain.
(Do not take it literals; if you put a mongoose in a toaster a stinky metal villain does not pop out).

Suddenly there was buzzing noise of great urgency. Knightkat (for it is he) nearly spilt his tea on his cravat. The biggest computer was flash and beep and make great alarm.

"Alert!
Alert!
Alert!"

It say in computer voice.

"Maiya.
Danger.
Danger."

On the screen was picture from Knightkat's secret camera which could show Knightkat all the streets of Moscow at once. (Sometimes Knightkat use it to see where traffic jams, but mostly he use it to save world). Now it show a scene of great frighteningness.

On roof of Presidential Palace in centre of Moscow
was evil Doctor Robogoose. Dangling from his evil claw
was helpless figure of beautiful Princess Maiya.

She had been kidnap!

*Here is beautiful Maiya. I look at this picture often –
I am sure her wink is for me!*

"This is case for Knightkat," said Knightkat.*

Before you could say "costumed crusader" Knightkat was wearing his Turbo-Charged Flying Cape and his 3-D Night Vision Mask, and was standing in the Knightkat Ejector Lift.

14

With a loud whoooooooosh that knock small grey figure off
his feet, the Knightkat Ejector Lift shot Knightkat up on
roof of mansion.

There, lighting up stormy dark sky was brilliant sign.

It was Knightkat sign!

It show world that Knightkat was on a mission.

Miles away in Meerkovo the bright light of Knightkat's sign woke everyone up. When they saw the sign, they say to each other: "It is Knightkat on a mission. Something dreadful must be happen". And they turned on their computermabobs to see what it could be.

Unfortunately the computermabobs is **CLOG!**

So they decide to go back to sleep and wait till morning.

Meanwhile, Knightkat sniffed the air, leaned into howling gale and swooped off roof and into the dark.*

15 Sec

10 Sec

5 Sec

KNIGHTKAT LAIR

*Do not try this at home. Without special equipment you will go splat on ground and be messy.

20 Sec

25 Sec

30 Sec

PRESIDENTIAL PALACE

16.66 MILES

It was very fast swoop; his **Turbo-Charged Flying Cape** make him travel at 2000 miles an hour, so he get to roof of **Presidential Palace** in only thirty seconds.

(Can you work out distance Knightkat fly to palace?)

There he discover hideous sight.

Doctor Robogoose was clutch poor Princess Maiya by her waist!

She was frozen in astonish and fright. The evil Robogoose was making roaring noise into the night, and waving the Princess's crown in triumphant.

Knightkat have to act quick before all is lost.*

Here we see how evil Dr Robogoose's hands are FILL with nastiness – but I think he is missing tin opener!

*This is extra thrillsy moment.
Music will go thumpy bumpy in film version.

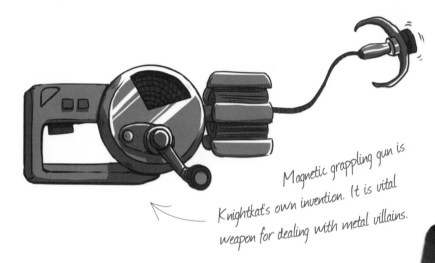

Magnetic grappling gun is Knightkat's own invention. It is vital weapon for dealing with metal villains.

He dive towards the wicked Robogoose and using his specials Magnetic Grappling Gun he fire the hook round leg of evil monster.

With all his strength Knightkat pull Robogoose off balance and he is hurling him into the darkness below. As he fall, Knightkat scoop Maiya into his arms.

It all happen very fast, and Maiya is breathless.

"You are safe now," Knightkat whisper to her. He felt
her heart tremble against his. And he see how the
wind make patterns in her beautiful soft fur.
As he flies off with her in his arms he is feeling
a little trembly himself.

As he puts her gently down Maiya reaches up
to him, moves his mask aside and is looking
lovingly at her rescuer.

"Aleksandr......"

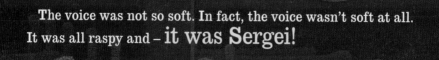

The voice was not so soft. In fact, the voice wasn't soft at all. It was all raspy and – it was Sergei!

At that moment, Aleksandr woke up. He find himself in his special Cravat Room and see Sergei looking up at him.

Sergei was looking all puzzlement. But Aleksandr drew himself to his full height (which was very high due to aristocraticness), and in instant became the entrepreneur businesskat and master of Orlov family mansion again.

His secret identity as saver of the world was secret still.

Aleksandr's Life Lesson

If you are force of evil and made of metal, you will be getting your comeuppance from force of good, made of fur.

#Extra mark for swotkat who know that Presidential Palace is 16.6 miles from Orlov family mansion!

Now read my other greatest tales

Available from all good bookshops

Also available to download as an ebookamabob
or audiomajig as read by the author – me!

For more information visit www.comparethemeerkat.com